spot

SPORTS

HOCKEY

by Mari Schuh

AMICUS | AMICUS INK

pads

puck

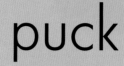

Look for these
words and pictures
as you read.

goalie

skate

The players are ready.
A hockey game starts.
Let's watch!

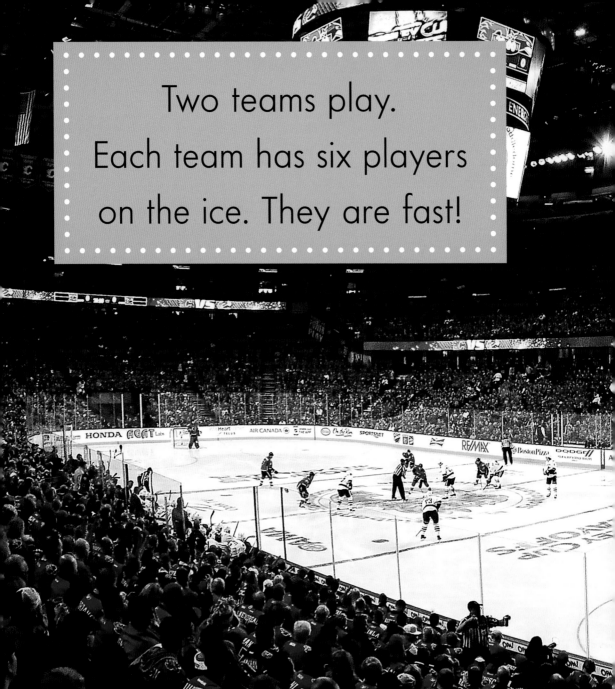

Two teams play.
Each team has six players
on the ice. They are fast!

Do you see the pads?
They are big and thick.

pads

Do you see the puck?
It is hard.
It is made of rubber.

puck

Do you see the goalie?
He guards the net.
He stops the puck.
Way to go!

goalie

Do you see the skate?
It has a sharp blade.
The blade is steel.

skate

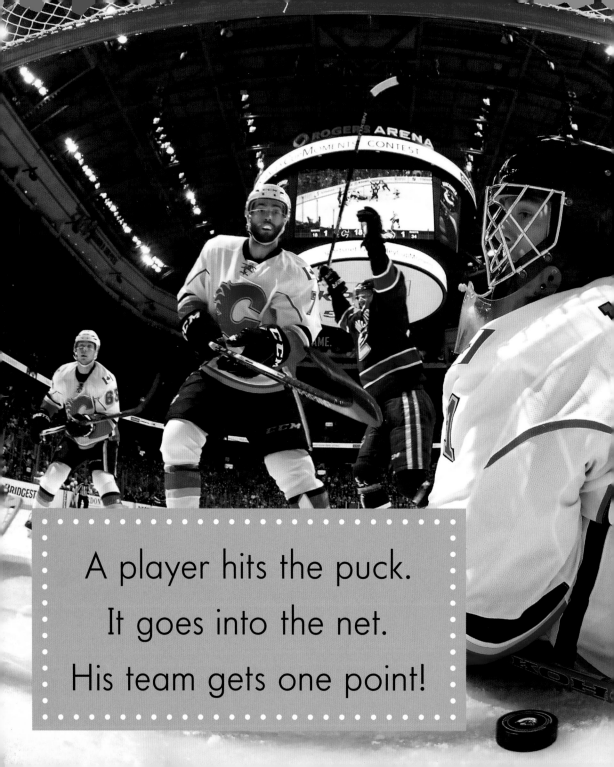

A player hits the puck.
It goes into the net.
His team gets one point!

Do you see the pads?
They are big and thick.
pads

pads

Do you see the puck?
It is hard.
It is made of rubber.
puck

puck

Did you find?

Do you see the goalie?
He guards the net.
He stops the puck.
Way to go!
goalie

goalie

Do you see the skate?
It has a sharp blade.
The blade is steel.
skate

skate

Spot is published by Amicus and Amicus Ink
P.O. Box 1329, Mankato, MN 56002
www.amicuspublishing.us

Library of Congress Cataloging-in-Publication Data
Names: Schuh, Mari C., 1975- author.
Title: Hockey / by Mari Schuh.
Description: Mankato, Minnesota : Amicus, 2018. | Series: Spot.
   Sports | Audience: K to Grade 3.
Identifiers: LCCN 2016057198 (print) | LCCN 2016058336
   (ebook) | ISBN 9781681510880 (library binding) | ISBN
   9781681522074 (pbk.) | ISBN 9781681511788 (ebook)
Subjects: LCSH: Hockey--Juvenile literature. | Picture puzzles--
Juvenile literature.
Classification: LCC GV847.25 .S37 2018 (print) | LCC GV847.25
(ebook) | DDC 796.962--dc23
LC record available at https://lccn.loc.gov/2016057198

Printed in China

HC 10 9 8 7 6 5 4 3 2 1
PB 10 9 8 7 6 5 4 3 2 1

Rebecca Glaser, editor
Deb Miner, series designer
Aubrey Harper, book designer
Holly Young, photo researcher

Photos by: Alamy Stock Photo/
Aflo Co., Ltd./Hideki Yoshihara,
1; Alamy Live News/MCT/
Philadelphia Daily News/Yong
Kim, 10–11; AP Photo/Mark
Humphrey, 3; AP Images/Icon
Sportswire/Rich Graessle, 6–7;
Getty Images/Derek Leung,
4–5, Doug Pensinger, 12–13, Jeff
Vinnick/NHLI, 14–15; iStock/cover,
8–9, 15

HOCKEY